LEVEL 2

Pandas

Anne Schreiber

NATIONAL GEOGRAPHIC

Washington, D.C.

For Lee Lee and Indy

Published by National Geographic Partners, LLC, Washington, D.C. 20036. All rights reserved.
Reproduction in whole or in part without written permission of the publisher is prohibited.

Paperback ISBN: 978-1-4263-0610-5
Hardcover ISBN: 978-1-4263-0611-2

Cover, 6, 13, 18 left, 19 right, 28-29 (all),: © Lisa & Mike Husar/Team Husar Wildlife Photography; 1, 22: © Katherine Feng/
Minden Pictures/National Geographic Stock; 2, 32 (top, right): © WILDLIFE GmbH/Alamy; 5: © Keren Su/China Span/
Alamy; 6 (inset): © James Hager/Robert Harding World Imagery/Getty Images; 8-9, 32 (top, left): © DLILLC/Corbis; 10-11:
© Eric Isselée/Shutterstock; 14: © age fotostock/SuperStock; 16, 24-25: © Katherine Feng/Globio/Minden Pictures/
National Geographic Stock; 17, 18-19, 32 (bottom, left): © Katherine Feng/Minden Pictures; 21: © Kent Akgungor/Shutter-
stock; 22-23 (inset), 32 (middle, right): © Carl Mehler/National Geographic Society, Maps Division; 26, 32 (bottom, right):
© ChinaFotoPress/Getty Images; 30-31 (all): © Dan Sipple; 32: (middle, left): © Kitch Bain/Shutterstock.

Special thanks to Kirsten Speidel, Assistant Professor of Chinese Language, Swarthmore College, for help
with translation and pronunciation.

National Geographic supports K—12 educators with ELA Common Core Resources.
Visit natgeoed.org/commoncore for more information.

Printed in the United States of America
Paperback: 19/WOR/12
RLB: 19/WOR/4

Table of Contents

Giant Panda!

Look! Up in the tree!
Is it a cat? Is it a raccoon?
No! It's a **Giant Panda!**

Giant Pandas can climb to
the tops of the tallest trees.
They live in the highest
mountains. They munch on
bamboo for hours each day.

Bear Cat

Giant Panda ————●

Black Bear

Pandas are about the same size as their black bear cousins, but their heads are larger and rounder. Also, pandas cannot stand on their hind legs like other bears do.

Pandas are a type of bear, but they seem more like raccoons or cats. In China, pandas are sometimes called *daxiongmao* (dah shee-ONG mah-oh), which means "Giant Bear Cat."

Like all bears, pandas are strong, intelligent animals with sharp teeth and a good sense of smell. Males weigh about 250 pounds and are about 4 to 6 feet long.

Pandas are great tree climbers. Sometimes they even sleep up in the treetops!

Bear Word

Habitat: An animal's natural home

Pandas have lived high in the mountains of China for millions of years. It is cold and rainy, but there are plenty of trees and a panda's favorite plant—bamboo.

Pandas used to live in more places, but today there is less open land with bamboo. Now pandas live in six forest habitats in China.

Panda Bodies

Pandas are black and white. This may help hide panda babies from predators, or enemies, in the snowy and rocky forest.

Their oily, woolly coat keeps them warm in the cold, wet forests where they live.

Hairs on the bottom of their feet keep them warm on the snowy ground.

Their black eye spots may help them look fierce.

Just like cats, pandas can see very well at night, when they are most active.

Pandas have large teeth and strong jaw muscles that are perfect for crushing tough stalks of bamboo.

Bamboo Breakfast

Pandas spend their day sleeping a little and eating A LOT!

Bamboo for breakfast, bamboo for lunch, bamboo for dinner, and bamboo to munch. What do pandas eat? You guessed it—bamboo! It makes up almost all of a panda's diet.

Pandas have to eat 20 to 40 pounds of bamboo each day to stay alive. It takes 10 to 16 hours a day to find and eat all that bamboo!

A Day in the Life

Pandas mostly live alone. But sometimes they hang out in small groups.

Pandas use 11 different calls to communicate with each other. They also leave their scent on rocks and trees for other pandas to find.

Bear Words

Communicate: To pass on information

Scent: A smell. Pandas use scent to communicate.

15

Baby Steps

Around August or September, a mother panda will find a den and give birth. Her newborn cub is about the same size and weight as an ice cream sandwich.

Panda cubs are pink, hairless, and blind at birth. They spend the day squeaking, crying, and drinking their mother's milk.

Soon, black fur will grow around the cub's eyes and on its ears and legs.

Cubs stay with their mothers until they are about two or three years old.

1.

In a few weeks, the mother can leave her cub to find bamboo. The baby cries less and is able to keep itself warm.

2.

When a cub is about eight weeks old, it will finally open its eyes. But the cub still cannot walk until it is three months old.

3.

When the cub is six months old, it can eat bamboo, climb trees, and walk around, just like its mother.

19

Red Panda

When people think of pandas, they are usually thinking of the Giant Panda. But did you know there is another kind?

Red Pandas also live in China as well as other parts of Asia. They eat bamboo just like black-and-white pandas, but they also love roots and acorns. Red Pandas only grow to be about the size of a cat.

The Red Panda has red fur and looks more like a raccoon than a bear.

Protecting Pandas

Today there are only about 1,600 pandas left in the wild. Many of the forests where pandas live have been cleared to make room for farms. Pandas have nowhere to go and no food to eat.

The Wolong (WOO-long) Panda Reserve in China is just one way people are trying to help. The 150 pandas that live there cannot be harmed.

0   500
Miles

C H I N A

□ Wolong Nature
Reserve

Panda Baby Boom

Pandas are also protected in zoos. The first pandas were brought to the United States from China in 1972. Today there are about 100 Red and Giant Pandas in zoos.

Q What do you get when you cross a know-it-all with a bear?

A A pan-duh!

In just one year,
16 cubs were born at the
Wolong Panda Reserve.

At first it was hard for Giant Panda moms to have cubs in zoos and on reserves. But in recent years, there has been a panda boom! Let's hear it for the cubs!

Earthquake!

In May 2008, a giant earthquake struck China. The center of the earthquake was right near the Wolong Reserve. Rocks the size of cars rained down from the steep mountains surrounding the pandas' home.

Now workers need to find new land for the pandas that lost their homes.

Bear Word

Earthquake: When the Earth's crust moves, it causes the ground to shake.

Panda-mazing Facts!

Did you know?

Ancient Chinese rulers kept pandas as their **pets!**

Pandas will **roll** around and tumble to get somewhere faster.

Pandas are very **shy** and will stay away from places where people live.

Q What do you get when you cross a playground with a bamboo forest?

A Panda-monium!

Pandas are **pink** when they are born! The color comes from their mom's saliva when she licks them. (Saliva means spit!)

Pandas can't run very fast, but they are good **swimmers** and great **tree climbers.**

Pandas can eat more than **22,000 pounds** of bamboo each year!

It takes **four years** to tell if a panda cub is a boy or girl.

29

Name That Bear

白豹

white leopard

白熊

white bear

猛氏兽

beast of prey

花熊

banded bear

Pandas can be found in Chinese stories and poems 3,000 years old! Over time, they have been called many different things. Which name do you think fits them best?

猫熊

catlike bear

熊猫

bearlike cat

白狐

white fox

大熊猫

great bear-cat

竹熊

bamboo bear

HABITAT: An animal's natural home

COMMUNICATE: To pass on information

SCENT: A smell. Pandas use scent to communicate.

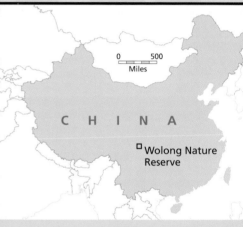

0 500 Miles

CHINA

□ Wolong Nature Reserve

RESERVE: Protected land area

CUB: A baby bear

EARTHQUAKE: When the Earth's crust moves, it causes the ground to shake.